Can I Tell You About...

Forgiveness?

CAN I TELL YOU ABOUT...?

The "Can I tell you about...?" series offers simple introductions to a range of conditions, issues and big ideas that affect our lives. Friendly characters invite readers to learn about their experiences, share their knowledge, and teach us to empathise with others. These books serve as excellent starting points for family and classroom discussions.

Other subjects covered in the Can I tell you about...? series

ADHD

Adoption

Anxiety

Asperger Syndrome

Asthma

Auditory Processing
  Disorder

Autism

Bipolar Disorder

Cerebral Palsy

Compassion

Dementia

Depression

Diabetes (Type 1)

Down Syndrome

Dyslexia

Dyspraxia

Eating Disorders

Eczema

Epilepsy

Gender Diversity

Gratitude

Loneliness

ME/Chronic Fatigue
  Syndrome

Multiple Sclerosis

OCD

Parkinson's Disease

Pathological Demand
  Avoidance Syndrome

Peanut Allergy

Selective Mutism

Self-Harm

Sensory Processing
  Difficulties

Stammering/Stuttering

Stroke

Tourette Syndrome

Can I Tell You About...

Forgiveness?

A Helpful Introduction for Everyone

Liz Gulliford

Illustrated by Rosy Salaman

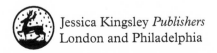

Jessica Kingsley *Publishers*
London and Philadelphia

First published in 2018
by Jessica Kingsley Publishers
73 Collier Street
London N1 9BE, UK
and
400 Market Street, Suite 400
Philadelphia, PA 19106, USA

www.jkp.com

Library of Congress Cataloging in Publication Data
A CIP catalog record for this book is available
from the Library of Congress

British Library Cataloguing in Publication Data
A CIP catalogue record for this book is
available from the British Library

ISBN 9781785925214
eISBN 9781784509101

Printed and bound in the United States

Manufactured by Thomson-Shore, Dexter, MI (USA); RMA24NS074, July, 2018

To Francesca, Edmund, Amelia and Rory

ACKNOWLEDGEMENTS

My attraction to the topic of forgiveness goes back many years. I first became interested in interdisciplinary perspectives on forgiveness during the course of my undergraduate degree in theology in the mid-1990s. An elective paper on "Psychology of Religion" opened my eyes to the psychological complexities involved in forgiveness, which complemented a fascinating theological paper on "Theories of the Atonement". I am grateful to Canon Trevor Williams, my tutor at Trinity College, Oxford, and to Dr Olivera Petrovich, who together kindled my enthusiasm for this subject, and inspired my MPhil on "Theological and Psychological Perspectives on Forgiveness".

I continued examining the theme of forgiveness when I became Research Assistant at the Psychology and Religion Group at the Faculty of Divinity, University of Cambridge and co-edited *Forgiveness in Context: Theology and Psychology in Creative Dialogue* in 2004.

CONTENTS

INTRODUCTION

Forgiveness is a complex and often misunderstood concept. As most adults know from experience, forgiveness is a far from simple thing to extend or accept. One problem is that the concept is often misrepresented. The adage "forgive and forget" has been particularly unhelpful in promoting the view that it is possible or desirable to forget a hurtful interpersonal offence. Of course, relatively minor transgressions can be overlooked – and often *are* – in the interests of maintaining social harmony. However, this oft-quoted saying lacks attention to the many contexts in which forgiveness is sought and for which "forgetting" may just not be possible.

The meaning of forgiveness is not often explicitly discussed in educational contexts, at home or in school. Young people pick up what forgiveness means from the examples they see, which might not always offer a very nuanced or helpful picture. Most of us are familiar with the experience of being encouraged – and sometimes even coerced – into saying we are sorry and into forced acceptance of such apologies. For instance, parents and teachers may seek to end children's disagreements with apologies all round, covering up the fact that in many cases it isn't a case of "six of one and half a dozen of the other". When we attempt to keep the peace this way, we reinforce a misleading and unhelpful message about what forgiveness is and what it achieves.

It is especially important for young people to learn about the complexities around forgiveness, such as whether it is always appropriate, and whether it might be best understood as a process that unfolds over time. It is important for parents, guardians, teachers and other moral educators to foster a critical approach to forgiveness to help young people understand when people might be saying sorry for manipulative and insincere reasons. It is irresponsible to promote an indiscriminate approach to forgiveness that could lay young people open to abuse and victimisation.

It is good to talk and encourage people, young and old, to reflect on forgiveness. *Can I tell you about Forgiveness?* is a guide for young people aged 7–13, their families, and their teachers and teaching assistants. To make reflection on the meaning of forgiveness more engaging, this book weaves considerations about forgiveness – what it is, and when it might and might not be appropriate – into a story about a boy called Joe and his family and friends. *Can I tell you about Forgiveness?*

has been designed to stimulate discussion about forgiveness in the home and in the classroom, giving young people the opportunity to reflect on the complexities of this important moral concept.

"Hello! My name is Joseph but my friends tend to call me Joe. I live with my mum and dad. I have a younger sister called Joelle, who is ten. People usually call her Jo too. It can get a bit confusing at times. I spend a lot of my time reading. I love books! I also like swimming, playing chess and cooking."

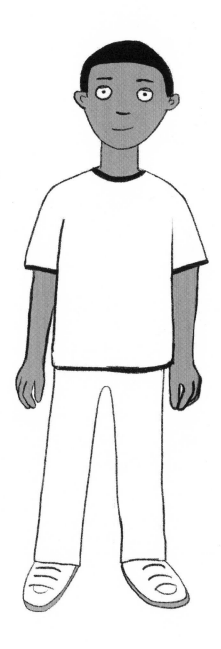

"Last week I told my friend a secret. I'm not going to tell you what the secret was because I don't feel I know many people well enough to share it. That's why I was confiding in my friend, Billy. I've known Billy ever since we met in Reception at primary school. Over the years, we've done a lot of things together and our parents have become friends too. Anyway, one of the days last week – I think it was Monday – I asked him if I could have a private word with him over lunch. I asked him not to tell anyone what I was about to tell him and he agreed. When I spoke to him he seemed to be very caring. He was listening carefully and he even asked me a question or two. I felt quite a lot better once I'd told him what was on my mind and I was glad I'd shared my secret with him."

"**A** few days passed. Imagine my shock and disappointment when, later that same week, one of my classmates came up to me during breaktime and made a comment that could only mean that Billy had told him my secret. I didn't know what to say in the moment because I was so upset that Billy had broken my trust in him. I would never have expected him to do that in a million years. I wondered why he had done it. After all, we've all reached an age where we know what the word 'secret' means, so it's not as if he didn't know what he was doing.

Billy and I are good friends – or, at least, we *were* good friends until this happened. My granny says 'forgive and forget' but I don't think I can put this behind me so quickly because I'm not sure how strong our friendship is now and whether I should trust him again. Perhaps Billy is sorry for what he did. It would be easier for me to forgive him if he were to apologise. At least I'd know that he was aware he had hurt me by betraying my trust in him.

I'm not sure I agree with sayings like 'forgive and forget' and another one I heard recently, 'least said soonest mended'. I think sometimes people *need* to say things and get things out in the open. To tell someone to 'forget' something that has angered them or hurt them just seems like nonsense to me. I suppose if someone accidentally jostled you in a queue and didn't say sorry, you might just want to 'forgive and forget' that, and move on. But if it's something more serious, I just don't think it's possible to 'forget' it. How can you wipe your memory of something like that? I'm not sure whether you can always forgive straight away either. I think forgiveness sometimes takes time – it's a process rather than a moment in time.

I'm very upset by what Billy did and, while I would like us to be friends, I need to tread carefully for the time being until I know whether he is sorry for what he did, and can see the effect his actions had on me and on our friendship."

"Of course, I'm no angel myself. No one is perfect. Everyone makes mistakes and behaves badly now and again. I think it's important to try to remember that when someone has done you wrong. I once took my sister Joelle's new football to the park without asking her permission first. I knew I should have, but at the time I told myself it didn't matter; it would get scuffed and dirty soon enough anyway and she would probably have said yes if I'd asked her. I knew I should have asked first rather than try to justify taking it, but I didn't and the whole episode ended really badly when I lost the ball...

I met up with some friends in the park for a kick-around with Jo's ball. Billy was there and a few other folks from school. We were playing quite near a fence that separates the playing field from some houses on the estate. Anyway, Lilya chipped the football and I headed it and it went over the fence and into someone's garden! I hadn't told anyone until then that the ball wasn't mine and that I had taken it without asking my sister first. When I told them the truth, there was a range of reactions. Some said it served me right for taking it without permission, while others were more sympathetic. Syed said he'd come with me to see if we could get it back, which was kind of him.

The problem was that all of the houses in the estate look very similar and we didn't know for sure which garden it had ended up in. We knocked on a few doors. Some people let us wait on the step while they checked their back garden but a lot of people seemed not to be at home. In the end I had to accept that I wasn't going to get the ball back. This would have been bad enough if Jo had known I had it, but it was even worse in the circumstances.

When I got home I admitted to Jo what I'd done and told her how sorry I was. Understandably, she was angry and disappointed in me, and so were my parents. I told her I would try to make amends for what I'd done; I'd use some of my birthday money (which was still in my piggy bank) and some saved-up pocket money to buy a replacement, and I assured her I would never take anything of hers again without asking first. Joelle could see how sorry I felt and how I would do all I could to put things right. She forgave me.

Although I gladly accepted Jo's forgiveness, for a while afterwards I still felt really bad about what I'd done and I couldn't forgive *myself* for it. It's a strange thing because I wasn't the person who had been wronged – that was obviously Joelle. But I think sometimes when we feel that we've let *ourselves* down we feel we need to forgive ourselves. Looking back on it, I think that feeling, along with our feelings of shame and guilt over what we did, helps us stop and think twice before we do something we know is wrong again."

"Joelle isn't perfect either – and neither are Mum and Dad, or anyone for that matter. Last night she and I were playing chess. Jo is two years younger than me so she hasn't been playing as long as I have. She's pretty good, though, and sometimes she beats me fair and square. However, yesterday she tried to win by cheating. We were about ten minutes into the game when I needed to go to the toilet. I had just moved a piece and so it was Jo's turn. I told her to wait for me to get back as I was only going to be a minute. However, when I sat back down she said she'd already moved one of her knights and she showed me where she'd positioned it.

There are two phenomenal chess players in our school club. One of them, Nadia, is in Year 13 and the other, Ariel, is in Year 11. Both of them can memorise where everything is on the board. Sadly, I'm not up to that standard yet, so I couldn't tell at first that something was wrong. However, as we resumed playing it became clear that Jo had allowed herself more than one move while I had been out of the room!

I had set up a good game and when I realised what had happened I was angry with her for having cheated. She denied it but I knew she had moved more than one white chess piece, even though I couldn't put my finger on exactly what she had done. We started to argue with each other and I called her a liar and a cheat.

At this point, Mum and Dad, who had been watching the TV in the other half of the sitting room, got involved in the disagreement. They tried to end the squabble. We had been making a lot of noise and it was obviously interfering with whatever they were watching on the television. They told us to say sorry to each other and to play together quietly and nicely. I was pretty cross about it because it was Jo who was in the wrong. She needed to say sorry for having cheated. I didn't need to apologise for anything!

I've seen this sort of thing happen at school.
Sometimes grown-ups ask everyone to say
sorry when they don't really know the whole
story. They assume it must be 'six of one and
half a dozen of the other' – and a lot of the time
it is. There are times, though, when one person
is clearly at fault and I don't think it's fair to
try to smooth things over by asking everyone
to forgive each other when not everyone
is to blame. I've noticed that adults might

occasionally do this with children, but they don't do it with each other. I think they know it isn't *always* six of one and half a dozen of the other but they say it because they think it will end the disagreement and get things back to normal.

If this is what Mum and Dad were hoping it didn't work. Jo said she was sorry but I could tell she didn't mean it. This is the thing about saying sorry – you've got to mean it in your heart or it doesn't count as a real apology.

I think everyone has been in the situation where they can tell that someone is saying sorry but doesn't mean it sincerely. You suspect they're saying it because they think it works like a kind of reset button on a stopwatch, and that once they've said the words everything can carry on as it was before.

I didn't say sorry to Jo because I hadn't done anything wrong, which she knew anyway. I told her that I would play chess with her again when I could tell she was offering a genuine apology. I also told her that in the end no one really wins anything by cheating."

"Of course, this business with the chess game isn't a big deal in what I've heard grown-ups call 'the grand scheme of things'. Even if Jo doesn't offer the sincere apology I asked for, I'll probably forgive her anyway because life is too short to hold a grudge over such a small thing. However, I don't think people should *always* forgive when people have done something very bad to them. For instance, last month it came to light that one of my friends (George) was being bullied at school, and had been a victim of this abuse for several months. By the time George's parents knew about it, he was scared to go to school.

It had all started a couple of months previously when the bully, Jasper, had started snatching George's crisps off him at lunchtime. The next thing was that Jasper was calling George names in the boys' toilets when he was sure there was no one else there to hear. He told George he was stupid. He told him he was ugly and that he hardly had any friends. Once he had got George to feel bad about himself, he said he would tell George's friends all sorts of lies about him, unless he handed over his lunch money.

George didn't have a large circle of friends and he was worried about losing them. He started giving Jasper his lunch money but it didn't make any difference. Jasper told George's friends that he'd been saying things about them behind their backs. It was all a pack of lies. One morning just as breaktime started, George burst into tears and told a teacher what was going on. A few of us were still in the classroom and saw him crying. He said he hated school because he hadn't got any friends and he was tired of having no lunch.

The teacher asked us to go to break while he talked to George. Afterwards he told us what had been happening. It was such a sad story. No one had realised what was going on because Jasper always made sure there was no one around to see him threatening George. As you can tell, I've been thinking a lot about forgiveness just lately. Should George forgive Jasper? I'm not sure it would be a good idea in this situation.

Bullying isn't like occasionally cheating in a game of chess or taking your sister's ball without permission. Bullying is extremely serious, and to forgive someone for doing it may make them think that they can get away with doing that to you or to other people again.

You have to ask why Jasper did it. In my mind, it's pretty clear that someone who feels the need to frighten, control and threaten other people has a problem. Perhaps they don't realise they have a problem themselves but that doesn't change the fact they do. Most people *don't* try to frighten, control and threaten other people to get what they want. Most people do not *abuse* other people in this way.

One of George's friends said we should all get together and give Jasper a taste of his own medicine, but I think revenge is a bad idea. Once victims start trying to get back at bullies, the things they do to each other just get worse and worse and a 'vicious cycle' develops. The other thing, of course, is that revenge just makes bullies of everyone. George was right to tell an adult about what was happening and now the bullying has stopped.

I feel so bad for George. It must have been awful to have been so terrified of going to school. There's a part of me that feels sorry for Jasper too. There's obviously something seriously wrong with his behaviour and no one wants to be his friend now. The school has arranged some kind of help for him from a psychologist. I hope it works for everyone's sake.

Although I feel some compassion and concern for Jasper, and maybe one day even George will too, I'm not sure George should think about forgiving him just yet. If Jasper comes to a point where he understands the effect of his hateful actions and says how sorry he is and promises never to do it again to anyone, maybe *then* George could think about forgiving him. But, in the end, it would be up to George to decide. After what happened, he might find it very hard to believe and trust that Jasper has really changed his ways."

" **A**lthough I haven't been targeted day after day by a bully, I can relate to the experience of having people tell lies about you behind your back. I think it has probably happened to most people a few times in their lives. Last summer I was working on a group project in Design and Technology with some of my classmates. Each group was given the task of making a raft which would eventually be used in a charity race from one end of the school swimming pool to the other. Everyone was really excited about it but people in the group had very different ideas about how to use the materials. In particular, there was a disagreement between me and one of the other members of the group, Alex, about the best way to build the raft.

The project went on over a number of weeks and I began to notice that other people in the group were ignoring me and giving me the silent treatment. Any suggestions I made were snubbed in favour of what Alex proposed. As I said, I don't believe in the saying 'least said soonest mended' so I asked one of the other group members why no one seemed to want to listen to my ideas. She told me that Alex had told them that I'd called them all 'muppets' and 'brainless idiots'.

I could see clearly that Alex had made it all up to get his own way, and I told my classmate that I hadn't said any of those things about anyone. At first I could tell she wasn't sure whether to believe me or not, but when I reminded her about the disagreements Alex and I had had a few weeks earlier, she could see that Alex's lies had been part of a manipulative attempt to build the raft his way. She explained to the rest of the group what had been going on.

It didn't take Alex long to realise the truth had come out when everyone in the group was talking to me again and we were all listening to each other. Tracy had a brilliant idea and we redesigned the raft, which went on to win the race some weeks later. I was still pretty upset by what Alex had done. Words can be very hurtful. There's no truth in the saying 'sticks and stones may break my bones but names will never hurt me'. Is there any truth in *any* of these old sayings, I wonder...?

51

Although Alex had deliberately set out to hurt me, I decided to forgive him. Both of us had wanted to design the raft our way and actually neither of us had the best idea how to do it! We were both being bossy and trying to dominate the group. Even though I forgave Alex, I still felt angry when I thought about his lies for some while afterwards. I guess forgiving someone doesn't mean that your bad feelings go away forever. Even now I find it hard to talk to him because those memories are still there. I suppose it may get easier over time."

"There was another time I was working on a music project with a girl in my class called Ciara. We were composing a piece together and the plan was to stay after school to use the music room. We got permission to stay late and were all ready to meet. I had been giving some thought to the composition at home and was looking forward to sharing my ideas with her.

On the day we were supposed to get together, Ciara didn't turn up. I couldn't understand it because I'd seen her in class, and she hadn't mentioned anything about not being able to make it over lunch either. At first I thought she was just a bit late, but after waiting for 15 minutes I could see that she just wasn't coming. I left school slightly concerned that something was wrong.

The next day I saw her in the playground before school. She was laughing and joking and seemed to be her normal, cheerful self. It certainly didn't look as if anything was the matter. I went up to her and asked her what had happened for her not to have met me as we had planned. She just shrugged and said she'd had a bad day at school and just wanted to get home.

I wasn't very happy about it, and I told her I thought it was disrespectful to have just sloped off like she did. She could have explained she'd had a bad day and we could have arranged to meet another time. As it was, she'd had me wait for 15 minutes for no reason other than that she couldn't be bothered to keep her commitment. Ciara said she was sorry and I accepted her apology. Everyone has a bad day now and again, and although it's no excuse for bad behaviour, no one is perfect, as I said before.

The following week we planned to get together again at 3.30pm, but on the day I was five minutes late getting to the music room because someone in the football team had stopped me in a corridor and asked me about the next match. When I got to the room there was no sign of Ciara. I thought perhaps she was a bit late as well, but when she still wasn't there after another ten minutes I started to think perhaps she had stood me up again. In the end, I gave up and went home.

The next day, Ciara glared at me as I came through the school gates. As I approached her she told me she was angry with me for not being there at the agreed time the day before. I told her I had just been five minutes late but she said it was no excuse and stormed off. She seemed to have forgotten that I had accepted *her* apology for not turning up at all the week before!

It seems to me that there's an important
link between being forgiven and forgiving
other people. If someone has forgiven you
for something you've done wrong, and you
are really thankful for it, that should change
you into the sort of person who forgives
other people when they make similar sorts of
mistakes, shouldn't it?

What do you think?"

NOTES AND KEY LEARNING POINTS FOR PARENTS, GUARDIANS, TEACHERS AND FACILITATORS

In this story, Joe reflects on his experience and understanding of forgiveness. Over the course of the narrative he reflects on whether you can always "forgive and forget", whether forgiveness unfolds over time, and whether it is a good idea to forgive people who have done something very hurtful. He also raises the question of whether you can "forgive yourself" and whether people are sometimes coerced into forgiveness to keep the peace – though that isn't a word he uses himself! Joe believes that the experience of being forgiven should change people, so that they become forgiving themselves. He is surprised that a friend he forgave for not turning up to an after-school meeting didn't forgive him for being just five minutes late the following week, and he questions whether she had taken his forgiveness on board gratefully.

The story begins with Joe wondering whether he should forgive his friend Billy for breaking his trust in him. He isn't sure what to do. Joe engages in some personal reflection and sees that he isn't perfect himself. He talks about a time when he stole his sister's football and lost it. Joe recognises that forgiveness is something you can give as well as receive. However, not all wrongs are equivalent and, as the story develops, Joe considers whether forgiveness is always appropriate. For instance, while he can easily forgive his younger sister for cheating in a game of chess, and gradually forgives a manipulator who told lies about him for his own ends, he isn't sure it is a good idea for his friend George to forgive a bully. He worries that to forgive someone for something so awful may make that person think that they could get away with doing it again.

Joe's story has been written to stimulate discussion about forgiveness in the classroom and at home, giving young people an opportunity to reflect on the complexities of this important moral concept.

KEY LEARNING POINTS

- *You can't always forgive and forget:* Joe heard
the adage "forgive and forget" from his granny.
He thinks it's simplistic. As he says, you might
be able to forgive and quickly forget someone
for accidentally jostling you in a crowd, but it
would be impossible to forget a *serious* wrong
even though you might, in the end, be able to
forgive it. Whether you can forget something
depends a great deal on what actually
happened.

- *Forgiveness is a process that could take a
long time:* Joe recognises that forgiveness
often happens gradually. He thinks he might
eventually be able to forgive Billy for betraying
his trust, and still finds it hard to talk to
Alex, because...

- *Bad feelings don't go away immediately:* Even
though you forgive someone you still have
memories about what happened that can spark
painful feelings. This doesn't mean you haven't
forgiven them. Difficult memories and the
emotions they evoke can't just be erased.

- *We all need forgiveness because we all make
mistakes:* When Joe thinks about the wrongs
that have been done to him, he also calls

to mind the wrongs he has done to other people, like his sister, Joelle. Joe recognises that forgiveness is both given and received. He believes that the experience of being forgiven should change people, so they become forgiving themselves.

- *We can show we are truly sorry for our mistakes by saying we are sorry and trying to make amends:* Joelle could see that Joe was really sorry for taking her football without permission because he apologised and was serious about trying to repair the damage by buying a new ball with his savings. When people can see we are truly sorry for what we have done and we do our best to make amends, people are more likely to forgive us because they are reassured that we understand we did wrong. Having said that...

- *Saying sorry isn't like pressing a reset button:* Although it is important to say sorry, it must be spoken sincerely and be accompanied by a commitment to change one's ways in future. Apologies should never be used to silence or manipulate other people.

- *Forcing other people to say sorry to keep the peace is wrong:* People should never be coerced into forgiving others. Moreover, relatively more powerful people (adults) should never try to force relatively less powerful people (children) into forgiving each other, especially when they don't know the full story behind a disagreement. This situation arose when Joe's parents tried to get Joe and Joelle to reconcile because the argument was interfering with their TV programme. It is important for parents, guardians and teachers to realise that they should not impose this practice on young people, as it is often done for the sake of convenience or to keep the peace.

- *Self-forgiveness:* It seems that self-forgiveness (ideally *in addition to* forgiveness from those we have wronged) is often important for people to move on. In the story, Joe felt bad about having taken his sister's football. He felt he'd let himself down and needed to forgive himself. Joe interpreted that feeling, along with feelings of shame and guilt over what he did, as a powerful way of making him think twice before doing something like that again.

- *Revenge is a bad idea:* Although forgiveness might not always be appropriate, Joe doesn't think revenge affords a better way of dealing with Jasper, who has been bullying George.

- *Compassion may be a possibility when forgiveness is not:* Joe hopes for everyone's sake that Jasper will change with the help he is getting. He thinks about whether he (and George) could feel concerned and sorry for Jasper in the future, even if George could never forgive him for what he did.

ITEMS FOR GROUP DISCUSSION

1. If you feel comfortable doing so, share a recent experience of forgiveness with the group.

2. How do we know other people mean the same thing by forgiveness as we mean ourselves?

3. What sort of things *can* be "forgiven and forgotten"?

4. Do people in different countries have the same understanding of forgiveness?

5. Would you have forgiven Alex for telling lies about you behind your back? Why/Why not?

6. Have you ever felt that someone was saying sorry just to "press the reset button"?

7. Have you ever felt that you needed to forgive yourself? What happened?

8. Do you agree with Joe that there's a link between being forgiven and forgiving other people?

9. Do you think Joe should say something to Ciara? What should he say?

FORGIVENESS AND DISCLOSING ABUSE

This book promotes conversation and discussion about the meaning of forgiveness. As such, it is possible that children may disclose sensitive personal experiences, such as bullying or other forms of abuse, as a result of engaging with these materials.

As an adult, it is important that you respond to any disclosures sensitively and supportively. If, after reading or discussing this book, a child reveals something to you, they deserve their faith in you to be respected and supported. How you respond can affect whether a child is likely to place such faith in someone again in future.

Any response to disclosure should be supportive. Bear in mind that it could involve a family member, and a child might feel that the act of telling anyone about it could land them in trouble. Remind them that their first loyalty has to be to themselves and their own well-being. For disclosures about bullying, neglect or any form of abuse, it is important to listen sensitively and take swift action by contacting an appropriate agency.

CONTACTS

UK

NSPCC: Addressing all forms of child abuse through practical interventions – www.nspcc.org.uk.

Childline: A children's charity set up to respond to crisis points of abuse and mistreatment from the child's perspective – www.childline.org.uk.

Young Minds: The voice of young people's mental health and well-being – www.youngminds.org.uk.

USA

Prevent Child Abuse America: Campaigning for great childhoods nationally – www.preventchildabuse.org.

Darkness to Light: A national organisation aimed at ending child abuse in the US – www.d2l.org.

RECOMMENDED READING AND OTHER RESOURCES/ AGENCIES AND HELP

Cantacuzino, M. (2016) *The Forgiveness Project: Stories for a Vengeful Age*. London and Philadelphia, PA: Jessica Kingsley Publishers.

Gulliford, L. (2013) "The Head and the Heart of the Matter in Hope and Forgiveness." In F. Watts and G. Dumbreck (eds) *Head and Heart: Perspectives from Religion and Psychology* (pp.273–312). West Conshohocken, PA: Templeton Press.

Noor, M. and Cantacuzino, M. (Art by Standing, S.) (2018) *Forgiveness is Really Strange*. London and Philadelphia, PA: Singing Dragon.

Watts, F. and Gulliford, L. (eds) (2004) *Forgiveness in Context: Theology and Psychology in Creative Dialogue*. London and New York, NY: T&T Clark International.

GLOSSARY

Abuse: (verb) to hurt or harm by treating badly, to use in a way that is harmful

Abuse: (noun) cruel treatment, harsh or insulting words

Apologise: (verb) to say sorry

Compassion: (noun) kindness, consideration and caring for others

Disrespectful: (adjective) inconsiderate, uncaring, without respect (see below)

Dominate: (verb) to control and take over by force

Manipulate: (verb) to control or shape something or someone for one's own purposes

Respect: (verb) to value, think a lot of

Vicious cycle: (noun) when an attempt to solve a problem creates new problems that are worse than the original problem